SUBLIME WORD:
FIFTY - THREE
WORKS OF LIGHT

MARCELLUS ANTHONY

Sublime Word: Fifty-Three Works of Light
Published by Marcellus Anthony Publishing

Please send your comments to the address below.
Thank you in advance.

vmbtf357@gmail.com

ISBN: 978-0-9967444-0-9

This book is available at quantity discounts for bulk purchases.

Printed in the United States of America.

Requests for information should be sent
to the above address.

Book Production: Marvin D. Cloud,
marvin@marvindcloud.com

SUBLIME WORD:
FIFTY - THREE
WORKS OF LIGHT

*"With all thy seeking, Seek Wisdom
and Understanding."*

What If?

What If the world was more than it seemed?
What If the world was as you want it to be?
What If the world was as you dreamed?
What If the things you desired, were within your reach?
What If your hopes and ambitions, were more than just wishes?
What If the things you seek, were also seeking you?
What If all the things you ever wanted, you could actually have?
What If I told you, there was only a price?
What If I told you, everything was within your grasp?
What If the cost, was only your Life?
What If it took, all of you to achieve it? All you had to do was actually BELIEVE in it.
What If you had to meet with Determination and Persistence, Motivation that's Consistent, Dedication and Commitment, Unyielding Faith that can break down any wall and Command everything within it?
What If it took, Singleness of Purpose without Procrastination? Your body, Mind and Spirit must be in Absolute Concentration.
What If you had to overcome your fears, and replace them with Courage and Love?
What If the world you lived in, Became more as you Loved?
What If the world and everything in it was yours? But it came with a price.
What If all you had to GIVE it, was your entire Love and Life??

Wisdom

Thanks to her I AM guided by her Light,
She guides me discreetly in all my affairs,
Thanks to her I have a fixed Vision and a strong Insight,
She whispers to me where I can only hear.

Thanks to her all things are made clear;
She Blesses me with a Sound Mind and an Attentive Ear;
Thanks to her I Understand things without conscious
Thought;
She permeates my Subconscious and guides me as I walk.

Thanks to her I see things with a new pair of eyes;
She exalts my Vision and I see all things from on High
Thanks to her my steadfast gaze brings my heart's desires
into fruition;
She Blesses me with Abundance and instructs me
through my Intuition.

Without her, I AM lost at sea;
Though my eyes search relentlessly, yet, I still can not
see;
Without her, what's within my reach I find with great
difficulty,
Though I labor with haste and vividly, my heart's true
desires and I never shall meet.

Without her, my efforts and wishes fall upon deaf ears;
I struggle day in and day out through each passing year,
Without her, all Hope and Faith are lost;
I say to myself, If I knew Life's wages I would pay it no
matter the cost.

With all thy seeking, seek Wisdom and Understanding;

To know the Truth, is to know Life's game is played
double-handed,
Which is played, is a matter of Choices;
If the right one is played, she smiles and rejoices.

Untitled

I will not fall
I will not stumble
I will not cripple
I will not crumble.
You can't touch me I'm untouchable.
You can't break me I'm unbreakable.
I have a fire you can't put out
I have a Light that won't go out
I will always see it through until my time runs out.
Stay focused; stay strong.
Strength, Power, Courage, Wisdom, and Faith is what I live on.
With Strength, there's Power
With Power, there's Courage
With Courage, comes Wisdom
And Wisdom brings Faith.

Mind

No sleep for the weary Mind
No sleep for the working Mind
No sleep for the wondrous Mind
No sleep for the thinking Mind.

It wishes, it dreams, it reflects its deeds,
Wrong or right, it's a reflection of sight,
For Good or for bad, it tests its might,
It destroys, it builds, it recreates, it fills, the entire space
around it, running rampant until it is stilled.

Seek the Silence, its indwelling home,
Seek the Silence, where all things are known,
Seek the Silence, where it attracts its own,
Seek the Silence, for it is waiting to be claimed and
owned.

A Traveler's Journey

From whence he's born, he is the Spirit made flesh
From whence he's born, he breathes Life's breath
From whence he's born, he knows no existence of fear
nor stress
From whence he's born, all he knows is Life's best.

As he travels, he grows into form
As he travels, he questions why he was born
As he travels, he meets with discouragement and his self-
made fears
As he travels, he learns and Understands the Truth, and
his appeared obstacles are made clear.

He seeks, he finds
He walks upon the Level of time
By Squaring his actions, he becomes One with Divine.
He asks, he receives
A Traveler on his Journey can accomplish anything
As long as he BELIEVES!
He knocks, it opens
He may enter with the right Token
While a Traveler is on his Journey, his Mind must always
remain open.

To know the Great Truth, is to have Faith to become Free
again
To know the Great Truth, is to always Give Hope to our
fellow man
To know the Great Truth, is to Give Charity to our fellow
man
To know the Great Truth, is to Seek to become One with
God once again.

Love

Try to Understand it, it confuses you
Try to control it, it breaks you
Try to hold it double-handed, it burns you
Try to withhold it, it haunts you.
It is the source of all things,
It is the origin of all things,
To have it dear and near;
Is the answer to all things.
Seek it,
Find it; but don't try to bind it
If you think you are in front of it
You are actually ten steps behind it.
Listen to its driving force
The way it is entertained is a matter of choice
To know its language is to hear God's voice.
It is silent at the same time loud
It is calm at the same time wild
It flows, it grows, it hides, it shows
The way you see it, nobody else will ever know.
Accept it
Embrace it
Its one true creed;
To become One with it is to live in Happiness and
Harmony.
No boundaries, no guidelines, no set of rules
To share it
To GIVE it
Is its only working tool.

You're My, I'm Your

You are my support;
I am your direction.
You are my reflection;
I am your obsession.

You are my balance;
I am your strength.
You keep me grounded;
While I keep you absent.

Of all your worries,
And all your fears.
Fret not the coming,
Of upcoming years.

Side by side,
We will accomplish All.
With God in between,
All obstacles will fall.

You are my fire;
I am your Light.
You give me Breath;
While I give you Life.

Chance

What is the difference between the successful and
unsuccessful man?
This one little thing;
This one little word;
It goes by the name of Chance.

One achieves, while the other daydreams.
The difference between them you ask?
This one little thing;
This one little word;
It goes by the name of Chance.

High Hopes,
High Fears,
The route you take,
Depends on the way you steer.
Once you take that Chance,
You'll become a Man,
Then your Vision is crystal clear.

Your Thoughts are things,
Your Dreams are real,
But only for those that work.

Have you heard this tale?
Have you heard this Truth?
That Faith is dead without Works!

What is the difference between the successful and
unsuccessful man?
One screams I can't,
One screams I CAN!
From Chance becomes a MAN!

The Road Together

As you travel down the path commonly less traveled,
Fret not Pure Heart,
We're on the road together.
As you struggle through your worries, your self-made fears,
Search within Sound Mind,
I Am always here.
In the middle of your doubts,
Second Thoughts and confusions,
Judge not according to appearances; they are nothing more than illusions.
In your time of great need,
Your most desperate hours,
BELIEVE your needs are met,
And they ALL will soon be ours.
While you're praying on your knees,
Hoping for things to get better,
Fret not little flock,
We're on the road together.

Journey Home

We're all on the same Journey;
But we are on different paths,
Some look forward to the future,
While other's mindset still reflects the past.

No matter how good or bad;
We must keep moving forward,
On our Journey Home,
There's Infinite Good to look toward.

We must keep our Mind's Eye,
Forever on the Most High,
He exalts our Vision,
And our Thoughts remain High.

Along the way we may get lost and confused;
During these times we are instructed to use our working
tools.
When we use our Imagination it grows stronger with
each use,
When it is controlled and directed there's no limit to
what it can do!

Along the way we meet with temptations and illusions,
If our Vision be steadfast we'll overcome such delusions.
To receive Life's best we must stand firm and be erect,
We may fall, we may stumble;
But we mustn't ever fret.

Know that such challenges,
Are nothing more than a test,
Throughout our Journey Home;
We are molded to become our best,

We must maintain an attentive ear
And a Faithful breast.

At the end of our Journey,
We'll meet with our Father once again at the throne,
All will be well,
And we'll be welcomed back home.

Let It Grow

A Giant lies dormant within; let it grow
With Unlimited Power and resources to win; let it grow
It's waiting to be awakened from within; let it grow
You are entitled to win from within; let it grow.
He is Abundance and plenty
His Blessings are many
Stress, fear, worry, or lack
He doesn't know any.
Calmness is power
Which makes Him strive
Love above all, towers
Which makes Him alive.
He's waiting to be called and commanded; let it grow
You have Infinite greatness within; let it show
Away with negativity and indecision; BE BOLD!
You have unlimited potential dormant within; let it grow!

Rise!

Rise! Rise! Rise!
We are not slaves of our environment or victims of
circumstance,
Do not be content and rely on other's Thoughts but
Think to become your own Man.
We possess God-like powers slumbering within if we but
seek to Understand;
"In the beginning, when God created the Heavens and
the earth," He did not create a slave, but a MAN!
In His Image and likeness,
We will discover "The Kingdom of Heaven Within" if we
but seek Enlightenment.
The constant cry over the ages has been to "Know
Thyself"
To search within;
We cannot fix external problems when the true cause
lies within.

Rise! Rise! Rise!
Has been the voice of the sages over ages,
"You are the Temple of the living God" are more than just
words put together on pages.
If all around you are bitterness and hatred;
Do not succumb;
Know that everyone's time is appointed and dated.

Rise! Rise! Rise!
We must Rise to the occasion;
NOW, is the hour.
Together in Unity;
The world is truly ours.
Organized and applied effort;
Is the meaning of Power.

Love is the beacon of Light;
Above all, it reign and towers.

Rise! Rise! Rise!
Is the chant now,
Calling ALL to be GREAT!
We must THINK things as we want them to be,
Simply dreaming is not enough
We must use our God-given gifts to ENVISION and
CREATE!
Soon enough, we will claim our birthright and be seated
at the throne;
But we must come together in UNITY on our Journey
Home.

Lift As We Climb

To reach a state that's Sublime we must Lift As We Climb!
To leave no one behind we must Lift As We Climb!
Lift As We Climb!
Lift As We Climb!
All is in One,
And One is in All,
Together in Unity we All stand tall.
All will be ours with the Power of Mind,
Lift As We Climb!
Lift As We Climb!
Make no mistake;
Building takes time,
Patience and Faith while we Lift As We Climb!
No presence of failure, worry or fear,
Lift As We Climb,
Will echo for years!
Know from within;
We have what it takes,
We may bend, we may tire,
But we never will break!
Lift As We Climb!
Lift As We Climb!
God is in Us,
We are in God,
It has been this way since the beginning of time.
Love is the Power,
The Power of All,
All is in One,
And One is in All!
Lift As We Climb!
Lift As We Climb!
Lift As We Climb!

The Current of Life

What we give our attention to we will see increased,
What we attract to ourselves is a matter of Belief,
The Current of Life;
Is a reflection of sight,
It gives us precisely what we choose to SEE.

Though, at times the waters be troubled,
Our debts be doubled,
It is a test to see,
If we'll Rise to be,
Or drown on our Current Level.

As we flow through Life,
We encounter doubts and strife,
To sink or swim;
We must choose our own fight.

The Current of Life;
Will test our might,
But to Understand its ways;
Is to live an Abundant Life.

We must confidently, cast ourselves into its streams,
Know that Plenty, are its means,
The Current of Life;
Will carry our Heart's Earnest Desires,
To the Isle of Dreams.

The Isle of Dreams

Is a place where some may never reach,
Some have faith but believe it's out of their reach,
They know it exists but think it rarely comes true,
But it's for those that take a leap of faith and pursue its route.

To some, it's clear as day,
To others, it is cloudy,
The heading you choose depends on your view,
Some shipwreck on their journey while others see it through.

Those that know,
And Understand its compass,
Will be guided through its darkest nights,
And sleep in Comfort.

Its beacon of Light shines as the rays from the Sun,
If you turn your back towards it,
You will struggle in the shadows,
And be fearful not knowing the outcome.

You can set sail and travel toward The Isle of Dreams;
Where Love, Health and Wealth are Abundance and Plenty,
Enjoy the oil of joy;
And live in Happiness and Harmony.

Or you can choose to believe it's a place nonexistent,
Live your years with resistance in contentment,
And wonder What If and how Life could be,
If you took that Chance and sailed to The Isle of Dreams.

To The Spirit of Man

The day you were born into the material world,
You became "the Word made flesh",
You are dormant within all men,
Once Awakened, makes all men their best.
The Spirit within Man;
Is the Father within,
To have a Pure Heart, then,
Is to have the strength of ten.
You are the master key to our heirship,
The inheritance to our throne,
You establish our Dominion over the earth,
And Comfort us on our Journey Home.
Once we acknowledge and recognize you,
You go before us and open the way,
Your Light radiates through us,
Which shines brighter than the brightest day.
To The Spirit of Man;
You are called to be Awakened,
To those still slumbering within;
Come forth!
You are called to command.
We will dwell together in unity,
And show forth His wonders,
We will Light The Candle and Sound The Trumpet for those,
Still dormant within in slumber.
Come forth!

Enemies Within

These enemies within,
Are common in the minds of men;
Doubt, Discouragement, and Distraction;
Breaks us all down from within.

Fear causes us to doubt,
For we are not certain of the outcome,
Discouragement halts our actions,
While distraction determines our outcome.

Failure may not be certain,
Depends on the way we start,
But failure is guaranteed;
If we never choose to start.

These enemies within;
Possess power only to the extent which we lend them,
They limit our possibilities,
Only to the limit which we allow them.

We must take back our power,
We gave to our opposition,
Once successfully done;
Our Heart's Earnest Desires will come into fruition.

We must evaluate ourselves;
To discover these enemies within,
Once we shed Light upon them,
We are surely entitled to win.

But do not be misguided,
It is no easy task,
It is for those with the Mental Discipline,
That are prepared for the task.

Old as Forever

There's something within us all,
That binds us all together,
It was present at our creation,
It is as old as forever.
To seek it is to find it,
It is everywhere present,
It has taught us throughout the ages,
It inspires us on pages.
To fill ourselves with it,
Is to be fulfilled without hatred,
To believe in its existence;
Is to live in its being,
To have Faith in its power,
Cultivates believing without physically seeing.
Once acknowledge and recognized;
All Good is ours,
Everything works in our favor,
And we make the best of each hour.
It connects us all together,
Which makes us depend on each other,
To see it in one another,
Is to Love as sister and brother.
It expresses itself through us,
Its Power is Divine,
Once we tune in on its channel,
We become One with Infinite Mind.
Its Infinite Supply;
Is old as forever,
We never travel alone,
It accompanies us on each endeavor.

It's Not For Me

What you view within produces the thoughts you think,
The thoughts you think makes the words you speak,
Be conscious of the words you speak,
Your heart's desires goes silent from the words;
It's not for me.
Temporary failure is not the same as permanent defeat,
Growth through struggle molds the man he must come
to be,
Many have faltered and faded away,
If they only knew success was a step away.
One must THINK success with every chance you take,
Without determination, persistence, and unyielding
faith;
Success within grasp slips away.
Your life is molded by the thoughts you think,
Be conscious of the thoughts you choose to speak,
One's dreams and aspirations will never come to be,
If you succumb to that destructive thought;
It's not for me.

Two Minds

It has long been discovered,
The duality of our Mind,
One is Conscious,
The other is Subconscious Mind.

Conscious makes choices,
While it consciously directs,
It relies off our physical senses,
And our common intellect.

It is limited by what we view,
With our two outer eyes,
Take away our senses,
And you've caught it by surprise.

It turns to our Subconscious,
With its Infinite ways,
Its source of power is from within,
Which is the cause of our ways.

Subconscious is the seat of our habits;
It can be cultivated and trained,
With unlimited possibilities;
It attracts what we claim.

It brings us our own,
Rather for good or for bad,
What we consciously feed it;
Is the result of our thoughts from the past.

The Conscious Mind directs,
And the Subconscious Mind follows,
Once they're on the same accord;
Success is sure to follow.

Circumstances

Many people blame their position in life;
Due to certain circumstances,
They are displeased with their current environment,
And wish for better chances.

They express their lacks,
Which multiplies their doubts,
They become overwhelmed with worries,
And desperately search for a way out.

Little do they know, the true cause lies within;
One cannot change outward effects by focusing on
effects,
They must start within.

Look to the Heavenly Father,
He dwells within,
Ask to receive,
The right way to see;
By thinking circumstances as we want them to be,
But first we must BELIEVE.

The more we GIVE,
The more we RECEIVE,
But we have to GIVE it first,
Know our needs are met,
And our circumstances are not meant to be a curse.

That which we describe;
We will see increased,
Choose to see the GOOD,
And live in Peace.

What we hold within;
Creates our circumstances,
Once we control what's within;
We'll control our circumstances!

Mental Discipline

Do you have it?
If not, it can be attained,
If you are willing to put forth the effort,
And endure the mental strain.
One must stretch one's mind,
And put it to good use,
With the Eye of your Mind;
There's no limit to what you can do!
Once harnessed and trained,
Through the aches and pains,
Mental Discipline will be yours,
And your mind you will claim!
If you desire riches and fame,
It can all be yours,
With the discipline of your mind;
You will always strive forward.
Through the Law of Use;
It gets better with each use,
Learn to subdue your passions,
And embrace the REAL YOU!
With Mental Discipline;
Anything is attainable,
You won't create excuses,
And always hold yourself accountable.
Mental Discipline is acquired in the Silence,
Though prior, its requirement,
That your body, mind, and spirit;
Be in total alignment.
Once you mentally determine to do something;
Stand firm behind it,
That perfect life is waiting for you;
Mental Discipline will help you find it.

Only Effects

Thoughts are causes;
Its results are effects,
Can you imagine everything we see are only effects?
Nothing but thoughts and ideas,
In physical form,
We were Blessed with the greatest gift the day we were
born.
We were created to create,
To be great is our fate,
Not victims or slaves;
That dread the coming days.
But a powerful being,
A little lower than the angels,
With a Fixed Vision;
Anything is attainable.
Can you picture it? Can you imagine?
Can you fathom, anything you earnestly desire you can
actually have it?
But it must be for Good,
For the benefit of all who's involved,
Mind is over matter,
But Spirit is above all.
Understand this Great Principle,
Then you are bound to Rise and stand tall.
Look around,
All we see are only effects,
Other's thoughts and ideas in physical form,
To use this Great Gift is to justify why we were actually
born.
To use it for Good,
In our lives and others,
Create our own masterpieces and share it with each other.
This world is truly ours;

To share with our fellow man,
Once we control the cause, what's dormant within;
We'll control what's without and effects will be at our command.

This world is ours to command.

Invisible Forces

Nature's most powerful sources are its invisible forces,
Same goes for man as he rises to command;
His invisible forces make him capable to become greater than;
Any other animal within our kingdom but his purpose first must be single.
To achieve his greatness, he must discover within what's latent;
Which was created long before time could actually be dated.
Thinking makes a man which follows right view,
His inner visional sense is what brings his thoughts into view,
Once Understood, you'll become conscious of what you choose to view,
What you view within, you are consciously or unconsciously attracting to you!
Your errors disappear once confronted by Truth,
Will you seek to Understand the invisible forces that dwell within you?
Understand the Great Law and put it to good use,
Thinking makes a man but it first starts from what you inwardly view.
To have Singleness of Eye is to become One with All-Mind,
Be steadfast in your Purpose then your conscious and subconscious will Harmonize,
Your thoughts will form and your ideas will be born for the world to acknowledge and recognize.

Self

To gloom or to glory,
We create our own story,
What we attract to our Self;
Affects our overall health,
Within and without,
To describe our Self doubt;
Diminishes us from within,
When its expression is protesting for an outlet out.
Know its presence is a present or a gift from within,
It can accomplish all things if we entrust it unto Him.
It attracts its own,
While it is calling us home,
The way it's decorated;
Is entirely our own.
The way we feed it;
It increases,
Which grows stronger with each use.
For good or for bad,
Depending on its use,
Self is always waiting for you to recognize you,
Strip down your external Self to discover the Self within
you.

Solitude

All throughout the ages it has been written to seek
solitude,
The Great Teachers and Sages taught it will help bring
clarity of inward view,
It cultivates a sound mind and allows you to discover
what dwells within you,
Understand your mental attitude is attracting every
condition towards you!

One must eliminate outside noise and seek solitude,
All power is from within which sheds Light upon its true
cause,
It brings peace of mind and your senses remain calm,
You bring forth what you believe which starts from what
you choose to view.

The world without is but a reflection of you,
What you give your attention to you will see increased,
Our greatest teacher spoke the undying Truth;
"According to thy Faith, so be it unto you."

Come to Understand the Universal Laws,
Solitude will help bring you closer to the Power of All
The Great Architect instructs us to Seek the Silence and
Be Still,
Believe you are in Him and He is in you still.

Thoughts Never Die

Thoughts are a spiritual activity,
Which the outside senses cannot not comprehend,
Therefore, the senses must be stilled;
Once stilled, one is filled from within.
They originate from the All Power, All Wisdom, and All
Understanding source,
The ones entertained or sustained,
Are completely left to the matter of choice.
Thoughts of old, to the thoughts of new;
All have potential to access the limitless possibilities one
can do.
Every thought that has ever been thought still exists
today;
From all the great teachers and sages throughout the
ages,
Yet, their thoughts still remain.
Therefore, thoughts never die;
The ones one chooses to recognize,
Will soon increase and multiply.
Where attention is directed;
The subject is revealed,
And Understanding appears,
Then one's Vision is made clear.

The Long Way

Some cut corners and search for the easy way,
They know not;
Growth and progress are established during the long
way.
If it was easily obtained overnight;
Just as easy as it came,
It can vanish out of sight.
To constantly avoid obstacles and challenges;
Is to overlook opportunities,
To use your Imagination and channel it.
The short route may be easy and convenient,
But the long way;
Builds your Determination and Resilience.
To seek the long way;
Is to travel the High Way,
Nothing beats the Experience and Knowledge obtained
along the way.
What is gained?
Depends on the road you take,
Choose the short way and its uneventful days,
Or travel the long way;
And gather all the precious jewels along the way.

Belief

We are all harvesting according to it,
To each its own,
In time, we're shown;
The nature behind it;
From what we reap it is known.

It attracts its own,
Like attracts like,
It produces its own kind,
Through The Law of Growth;
It must bring forth after its state of mind.

It causes us to see,
Through its own lens,
Wherever the focal point may be,
All gathers to support,
And everything falls to command.

It creates its own thought,
Which suggest another like thought,
The power it brings,
As unimaginable it may seem,
This True Gift of God;
Can never be bought.

Though, environment may contradict;
All you hold within,
As your harvest grows;
In time, you'll see;
You mustn't let your surroundings affect your Belief.

Passion

Once discovered is to be uplifted,
And live in eternal joy,
But if not harnessed and directed;
One can be consumed and destroyed.

Balance must be met,
For controlled chaos to be kept,
It can sway you every which way,
And drain you til there's nothing left.

It is derived from within,
Where All Power begins,
To discover its hidden realms;
Is to be born again from within.

A Conscious Awakening

It is already happening among the vast,
For those that know, troubles won't last,
Become conscious of your conscious;
Which opens the channel to your Subconscious,
Once successfully done;
You'll begin to accomplish all things without much
consciousness.

Have you seen this mental chemistry?
It is occurring all about you,
Remove the hoodwink from your eyes;
And discover the Light all around you,
Once acknowledged and recognized;
You will speak with a new tongue and no longer rely on
your two outer eyes.

It is bringing forth greater Understanding and a deeper
Insight,
It's instilling a sense of power and the Will is its might,
Its trumpet has sounded,
And its fire glows bright,
It is calling All to walk by Faith;
And not by sight.

No More, No Less

We cannot expect that which we do not give,
We get out of life what we put in,
Do you want life's best? Then give life your best!
In turn you'll receive;
No more, no less.

What happened in the past, let it go;
It's irrelevant,
Live in the Now and be filled with benevolence,
Or give your Attention to stress and receive more stress,
The Law is the same;
No more, no less.

Do you Desire more strength?
Make good use of your current strength,
While Believing you are Highly Favored;
And Blessed by the Best,
In turn you'll receive to the extent which you give,
But always expect the best;
No more, no less.

A Bar Too High

High standards and high hopes;
Can create high doubts,
That feeling we don't have what it takes;
Breaks us down from the inside out.
It discourages the Spirit;
And causes us to fear it,
We feel we are far off;
And it's impossible to get near it.
Our conscious tells us the bar is too high,
It limits our abilities to take a chance and climb,
If we but still our conscious, our subconscious will rise,
We will see things clearer and begin to take possession
of our minds.
Is there really such a thing as a bar too high?
If you Believe God is in you;
You can never aim too high,
All is needed is that you Concentrate your Attention;
On one step at a time.
Soon, that bar too high;
Will be just another stepping stone,
Keep moving forward;
With your Vision on the goal.

Light The Fire

We have an obligation to become better,
Do well to others in hope to inspire,
For those that still dwell in darkness;
Light the fire.

Let the Light shine through you to guide others along the
way,
Know from within we all have what it takes,
To achieve our own greatness and fuel our Burning
Desire,
Light the fire.

In the silence of darkness and the glory of Light;
Light the fire for those that fight the good fight,
Aspire to inspire and be the electrical wire;
To spark the Divinity in others and to always strive higher.

There's no limit to one or a limit to all,
The power of One is the power of All,
Be still and fulfilled from within is what He asks and
requires;
Light the fire.

Be the searchlight for those still lost in the forest,
Be grateful for the teachers that lit the fire before us,
Know the Creator of the Universe is always conspiring for
us,
Now, light the fire for fellow travelers and brotherly
explorers.

Locked In A Cage

Many lives are spent unconsciously locked in a cage;
They know not the cause of their silent rage,
Their eyes are blinded by their inward hate;
Once judgment is clouded, they become doomed to their fate.
No direction or progression leads to a downward slope,
Yet, the inner visional sense attempts to stay aloft;
The conscious sustains any breath of hope.
While Life remains, it constantly feels choked
The thoughts entertained, feed their silent rage;
Which grows stronger with each passing day,
Even though, they possess the key to their own cage;
The ability to free their mind and discover their own way;
Instead, they cling to the bars of their self-made cage,
Hate, anger, doubt, worry, stress, and fear;
Hastens their decay.
In due time,
They'll become free so they sit and wait,
Their body roams the world;
While the Spirit is locked in a cage.

Be Not Afraid

Are you afraid? Do you fear not knowing the outcome?
If things don't go as planned;
Are you thrown into frustration and worry how come?
Understand some things are beyond our control,
Seek our Unseen Ally for Comfort;
And to be consoled.
Even though, at times the waters are high;
The night is filled with terrors,
And nothing but gloom meets the eye,
Be not afraid
Think of things as you want them to be;
Not as they are,
Exalt your inner visual sense,
To become as you want to be;
Not as you are.
To improve yourself;
Is to improve the world without,
The better you become;
Is to help change the world from the inside out.
Be not afraid
Of your daily worries or your doubts,
Overcome your fears by transmuting them to Courage
and Love,
Let the Light in to draw the darkness out,
Believe the Great I AM reigns from above;
Let Him guide your every step and lead you to Eternal
Love.

Take It All

As far as we know;
This Journey of Life is a one way trip,
All the experiences you've ever had;
The good, the bad, happy or sad,
Take it all;
Regret nothing from your past.

They build you up,
Some break you down,
Others leave you twisted all around.
But if your heart is beating;
You're still here for a reason,
Take it all in and keep on breathing.

Press on and keep moving forward,
There is always some Good;
To keep striving toward.
You may stumble,
You may fall,
It matters not;
Take it all.

Face it and embrace it,
But don't ever stoop to hate it,
If you don't want it;
Don't think it,
Don't bother to ever say it.

Be blind to all evil;
Give them no sight,
There's a power within;
Whose Will is its might.
Take it all in and keep your grip tight;

You will win from within,
And He will fix your every fight.

At The End Of The Tunnel

In the tunnel;
It's dark, cold, lonesome, and doubtful,
Every step moves with uncertainty,
Each breath exhales frantically,
While the voice within whispers;
Follow me.
Contradicting thoughts start to rise,
Reaching for the walls with closed eyes,
Racing heart with trembling hands,
Stuttering steps and a wavering stance.
But something grabs hold of a hand;
It's firm but gentle which erects the stance,
As the eyes open;
The Vision is fixed,
Upon an illuminating Light that brightens the pit.
Every step moves with confidence,
Each breath is calm and relaxed,
Thoughts are stilled and the heart beats with zeal,
Closer to the Light;
The warmer it feels,
The hand releases and the voice within whispers;
You have arrived;
At the end of the tunnel.

Instrument

What is your instrument? Have you discovered it?
If not, seek it!
Find your expression;
The Great I AM works through all things,
And comes as Intuition.

Universal Mind;
Whose Power is Divine,
Omniscient, Omnipresent, and Omnipotent,
Is within you all the time.

It is developed through Mind;
Though, static and sporadic,
Thought makes it dynamic and systematic,
Once constructively harnessed and directed;
Anything you earnestly want;
You can have it!

First, you must seek your Instrument;
The channel you and Him Harmonize,
Our Unseen Ally will guide you,
But you must yield to Him and His Word abide by.

Your mind must be cultivated and receptive;
To receive all of His signs,
"You are the Word made flesh"
Know from within you are Divine.

Take no credit,
And give Him all the glory,
Understand the day you were born;
You were bound for a glorious story.

Creators

We become what we create,
From our Power that's innate,
Once we see it then we think it;
We mold it into shape.

It is a spiritual activity,
We use it every day,
Conscious or unconscious;
We're attracting what we say.

If you're thinking;
You're creating,
Which can go either way,
Constructive or destructive;
Depending on your clay.

The nature behind it forms it,
It produces after its own,
Every Mind is attracting;
To it its very own.

Become conscious of what you view;
You'll think, speak, and act the same,
In order to create your world without differently;
The way you see it and think must change.

We are all Creators;
With our own Master Work,
Search within and find Him;
Then put His Will to work.

The Great Architect will guide you;
Entrust Him and Believe,

The things you seek will find you;
But you must be able to SEE.

Those Who Dream

For those who dream;
Nothing appears as it seems,
What's behind their eyes;
Is only understood by those who dream.
Some drift and wallow,
Few dream and follow;
The world's omens that are placed all around,
Some fear to fly,
While others fear to drown.
They suffocate their dream,
With their doubts and fears in between,
They know not the cause;
Of their destructive flaw.
Understand the Law;
Then rise above all.
Do you know within who you truly are?
A powerful being with unlimited resources,
This world is yours and molded by your choices,
They originate within;
From those who dream,
Overcome what's in between,
And live as you dreamed.

Look Up!

A downward gaze precedes a spiral haze,
It creates negative conditions and traps your mind in a
maze,
Though, your outer eyes are looking forward;
Your sight is still dazed,
Look Up!
Is the cry from our begotten sage.
When all around you are shadows,
And darkness cover your days;
It is nothing more than the absence of Light,
Look Up!
Then the Great I AM will fight your fight.
But you must put forth the effort;
To establish your faith,
Blot out negative surroundings and they'll soon be
replaced;
See yourself in favorable conditions to receive a higher
estate,
Look Up!
Above the clouds and see God's face.
To dwell in negativity;
Is to see it increased,
Envision Abundance and Prosperity,
Genuine Love will bring you Peace.
To increase beatific conditions;
His Word, take heed,
When all hope appears to be lost;
Look Up!
And Believe.

A Mother's Strength

Its endurance is unbreakable,
Its faith is unshakable,
Its Love is heaven sent,
Nothing can compare;
To a mother's strength.

It's fulfilling and revitalizing,
Its beauty is hypnotizing,
It's unwavering and unyielding,
To be in its presence;
Is an ineffable feeling.

It holds no boundaries,
It knows no limits,
It goes beyond its means,
And sacrifice its dreams,
To provide nothing but the best;
For its beloved offspring.

Its determination does not wince,
Its perseverance stretches beyond length,
Out of all the things in the world,
Nothing can compare;
To a mother's strength.

See The Good

Curse nothing but Bless All,
If negativity appears;
See the Good,
Which is All,
Then wish it well;
To watch its power fall.
Error disappears when Truth appears,
Good is everywhere present;
Gain wisdom from every experience to make it a valuable
lesson;
See that everything you receive is disguised as a Blessing.
When things don't go your way;
Know there's a better way,
Once you see the Good in All;
More Good will come your way.
Lift the Eye of your Spirit,
It'll bring Light to your two outer eyes,
Understanding will increase,
And you'll be raised from your current state,
Then from there, continue to rise.
Everything works in your favor;
As long as you believe it should,
It matters not the circumstances,
Remember to always see the Good.

The Narrow Gate

How narrow is the gate;
That few choose to travel,
Believe and have faith;
You are the Creator of your fate.

Though, the path is rugged and wedged;
Press on and forge ahead,
Endure the trying times;
Keep your vision steadfast and sublime.

You will meet with temptation and uncertainty;
Do not be deceived by illusions,
See beyond the mirage;
Do away with such delusions.

The narrow gate is scarce;
Not many follow its path,
Majority search for the gate that's wide;
It appears easy enough to climb,
They lose sight of the narrow gate;
And remain slumberous inside.

So Is He

What a man most frequently and intensely thinks;
He becomes,
As he repeatedly thinks it in his silent hours;
It will become.
Where he finds his treasure;
Is where his heart is,
What he receives from life;
Depends on where his directed thought is.
As he gives to others;
He receives in kind from Universal Mind,
What he holds underneath;
He will soon come to be,
Whatsoever he thinks in his heart;
So is he.

The Law of Love

Yet, it remains;
And it always will,
To harmonize with it;
Is to understand The Great Architect's Will.
For those that know;
Knows its language,
Give without expecting;
Forgive without being tainted.
It is only seen;
By the Eye of Truth,
Once you abide by it;
It will become obedient to you.
Remove your shackles and subdue your passions,
Deny yourself to come into fashion.
Be of service to others all around you,
The Law of Love;
Governs and bounds you.
Where you place your love;
You place your life,
You'll find your Self;
Through struggle and strife.
Keep your thoughts high,
With a watchful eye,
The Law of Love;
Leads to Eternal Life.

Time Spent

Do you ever think about your time spent?
Wonder about life,
And where it went?
Are there things from the past that kept you from the
dreams you once had?
Are you filled with regret?
While you constantly doubt and continuously fret?

If so, doubt and worry kills,
Even worse from within;
You are liable to create mental ailments;
And sickness from within.

Impure thoughts brings forth impure conditions,
Give Light towards these enemies and remove them for
good.
You were created in a perfect image;
Everything about you is Good.

The time you've spent directing thought towards
negativity;
Take back your Power and free your Mind from captivity.
Once successfully accomplished;
You'll live in the now and enjoy your days at length,
You will make the best of each moment;
And Love your time spent.

Plant The Seed

If thoughts are causes,
And conditions are effects,
The thoughts we choose to entertain;
We will soon enough get.
What we sow;
We shall reap,
Harmonious or inharmonious;
Depending upon the seed.
We can't plant the seed of one,
And expect to bear fruit of another,
What comes out of our mouth each time;
Originates from our Mind.
Are you conscious of the seed you plant?
The Law holds no respect to person;
We harvest what we choose to grow,
Whatsoever seed we choose to plant;
In the world without,
It is bound to show.

Just Pray

Spirit is the Driving Force of the Universe;
In it we live and move and have our being,
Do not think, but have faith;
It cultivates believing without physically seeing.
How does one establish faith?
Just pray;
The Great I AM will go before you and open the way.
Seek the Silence in solitude,
Ask to receive your heart's earnest desire,
Believe your need is met and make the best of what you have;
While consistently striving to aim higher.
If there are unsatisfactory conditions?
Just pray,
When all is well?
Just pray,
The works that will be done;
Is according to your faith,
If you desire to establish your rightful heritage;
Seek the Silence and just pray.

Walk Slowly

A great many moves in a scurry,
Their mind runs rampant;
They are always short on time,
And live in a hurry,
Majority tend to overlook opportunities;
Compared to those whom walk slowly.

Thoughts are jumbled,
Days are chaotic,
Mental in disarray;
Everything's out of place.

Confused by their actions;
Unconscious of their mental state,
Repeated in mind;
I can't afford to be late.

Understand, calmness is power;
Develop repose,
Begin to walk slowly,
Keep your conscious thoughts on hold.

Smell the roses,
Give Love wherever you go,
Keep your vision upward,
Let your inner Light glow.

Take your time;
To breathe Life's Breath,
Be fulfilled within,
And discover your Real Self.

By squaring your actions;

You always give your best,
To seek what is Holy;
Keep your thoughts high,
Walk slowly.

Light Beyond The Shadows

How long will you fight?
How long will you endure?
The shadows of the night;
Entices and allures.

There's dawn beyond the night,
Light beyond the shadows,
Once your courage is tested by might;
Will it stand upright,
Or prove to be hallow?

Be steadfast in your belief,
As the waters flow above and underneath,
To see the dawn beyond the night;
Endure the shadows with its fright.

See towards victory,
Though, not in physical sight,
How triumphant it will be;
To fight until the morning Light!

I See You

I See You; the presence that permeates all things
I See You; free, flawless, and triumphant which transpires
from the unseen
I See You; fearless and confident who establishes my
strength
I See You; compassionate and kind whose Love is heaven
sent.
I See You; humble and meek,
Who freely gives forth His Abundance;
If I only look to seek.
But if I turn my back towards you;
There will be "wailing and grinding of teeth"
I will spend my days in darkness
Shadows and I will continually meet.
The choice is mine on what I choose to see,
I choose to acknowledge and recognize The Supreme
Architect,
His Free Spirit,
Guides and directs my feet.
I See You!

"The Light of the world is the Love of God and the Word of Christ."